D1591538

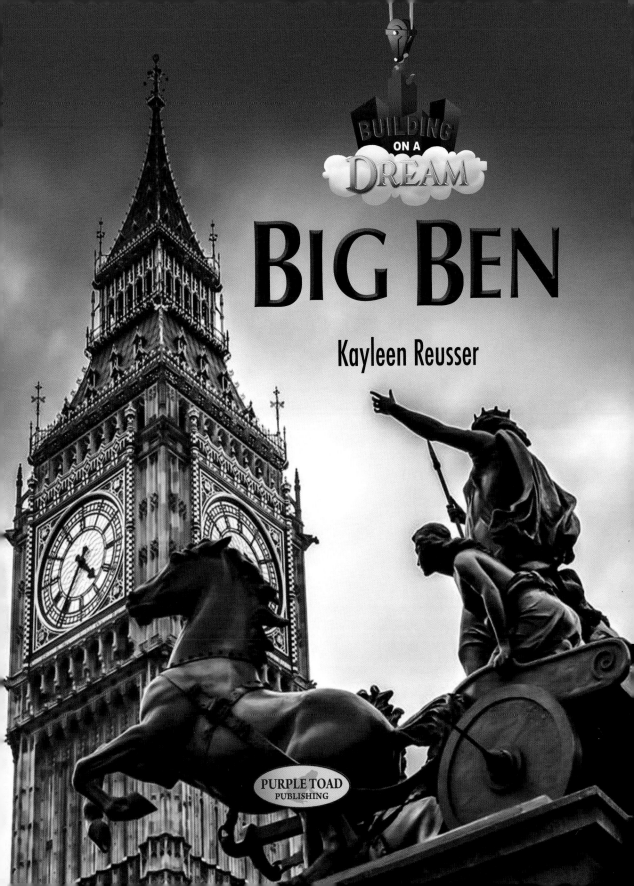

Building
ON A
DREAM

BIG BEN

Kayleen Reusser

PURPLE TOAD
PUBLISHING

PURPLE TOAD
PUBLISHING

Printing   1   2   3   4   5   6   7   8   9

Big Ben
The Eiffel Tower
The Space Needle
The Statue of Liberty
The Sydney Opera House
The Taj Mahal

Publisher's Cataloging-in-Publication Data
Reusser, Kayleen.
  Big Ben / written by Kayleen Reusser.
    p. cm.
Includes bibliographic references, glossary, and index.
ISBN 9781624692017
1. Big Ben (Tower clock)—Juvenile literature. 2. Architecture—Vocational guidance--Juvenile literature. I. Series: Building on a Dream.
 NA2555 2017
 507.8

Library of Congress Control Number: 2016937176

eBook ISBN: 9781624692024

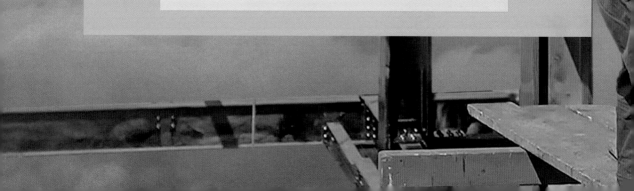

ABOUT THE AUTHOR: Kayleen Reusser has written more than a dozen nonfiction children's books. She enjoys learning about other cultures and sharing that information with children and adults through writing and speaking. She lives with her family in the Midwest.

CONTENTS

Chapter One
King of Bells 5

Chapter Two
A Great Clock 9

Chapter Three
Try, Try Again 13

Chapter Four
Big Ben Rules 17

Chapter Five
Long Live Big Ben! 21

Chronology 26

Chapter Notes 28

Further Reading 29

Works Consulted 29

Books 30

On the Internet 30

Glossary 31

Index 32

During Queen Victoria's reign of England, the biggest bell in the world was made. It was called Big Ben.

King of Bells

Ba da rump! Ba da rump! Ba da rump!

The hooves of 16 white horses clattered against the wooden floor of London's Westminster Bridge. The October day was bright and warm. Red, yellow, and brown leaves from nearby oak trees fluttered to the ground under the horses' feet. The crowd that had gathered in New Palace Yard paid no notice to Mother Nature's beauty. They rushed forward as the team pulled its heavy load to a stop.

Fweet! Police officers blew sharp whistles. The sounds meant, "Stay back!" The heavy item on the wagon weighed 16 tons (32,000 pounds). An accident could mean certain death![1]

The crowd shuffled away, disappointed. They had waited 20 years to see the item on the wagon. In 1856, people in London did not see many surprises. This was a big one!

The item, standing 7 feet, 6 inches tall, looked like a giant. It was not a weapon like a cannon that could help defend England from attack, although someday it would help the British people win a war.

Nor would Queen Victoria, who ruled England, want the huge, plain item in her palace. Yet someday every town and village in Europe would want one like it.

So what was this fantastic item that stood so tall and measured 9 feet around?[2] It was a bell—the biggest and best in the world. Its name was Big Ben.

Big Ben had been made in a large foundry in the village of Stockton-on-Tees. A foundry is a place where hot metal is molded into shapes. In August 1856, workers used two ovens to make Big Ben.

The bell completed

They poured a hot liquid mixture of tin and copper into the huge mold. Two days later, the mold had cooled. Workers in the foundry gathered around Big Ben in amazement. No other bell in England, maybe the world, was near it in size. The closest was Great Peter in the cathedral of York Minster, which weighed 12 tons.[3]

Carefully, Big Ben was lifted to a cart and placed on a train car. Straps held it firmly in place as the train carried Big Ben to the harbor of Stockton-on-Tees.

The roads from Stockton-on-Tees to London were rough and uneven. The people who had made Big Ben believed the rutted roads would damage the bell during the long trip. Traveling across water on a ship to London would offer a smoother ride, they thought. A schooner named *The Wave* was chosen to sail with Big Ben to London.

Sailors cautiously unloaded Big Ben from the train. They gasped at its great size and weight. Slowly, they lowered Big Ben onto *The Wave*'s deck.

Moving Big Ben was challenging.

Crash! The bell sank through the boat's floor. The owner of the foundry had not followed the directions for making Big Ben. The great bell was to weigh no more than 14 tons. Big Ben weighed 16 tons—four thousand pounds over the limit.

Big Ben was created in a foundry in the village of Stockton-on-Tees.

It took weeks for the boat to be repaired with a stronger floor.[4] When the boat finally set sail, Big Ben was on board, but its problems were not over. During the voyage, *The Wave* was caught in a bad storm. The boat jerked like a rocking horse as huge swells of water crashed over its sides.

The people of London heard about the ferocious storm from other boat captains. When *The Wave* didn't appear in London on the day it was due, they worried. Weeks passed. Each day the people looked across the harbor, hoping to see the sails of *The Wave*. Had the little boat survived the storm? Would *The Wave* and Big Ben arrive safely?

By October 1856, nearly everyone thought the boat, its crew and Big Ben had been lost at sea. That was the fate of many boats caught on the ocean in bad storms.

Just as the people were ready to give up hope, they spied movement on the horizon. It looked like a small ship. As the object crept closer, the viewers strained their eyes, hoping to catch a glimpse of the ship's flags. Finally they could tell it was a British ship. Could it be the boat they had been looking for?

Sir Benjamin Hall

After it burned to the ground in 1834, the palace was rebuilt.

A Great Clock

Strong sailors tied ropes from *The Wave's* bow to the pier. The little boat had finally arrived in London harbor! Slowly, carefully, the sailors moved Big Ben to a wagon pulled by strong horses. Then they drove their gigantic cargo across the city to New Palace Yard.

The plan was for Big Ben to be displayed in a new building on the bank of the River Thames (**TEMS**).[1] The building would be called the Palace of Westminster. It was the second one built with that name.

In 1834, two careless workers in the old Palace of Westminster had left a hot furnace unattended. The building caught fire and burned to the ground. It was a sad loss to the British people. Government leaders had been meeting there since the year 1200.[2]

The people of London wanted to build a new government building on the same spot. The new building would contain two things: a clock tower and bell.

For hundreds of years clock towers in village squares had been important to the people of England. When a bell was rung, people knew something important had happened. A baby had been born or someone had died. A house was afire or an enemy was approaching. People knew when it was time to attend church or school by listening to the bell.

Many bells were given names. Church bells were often named after the church where they hung. The bell that hangs in St. Paul's Cathedral in London is called Great Paul.

Ben Caunt

No one knows how Big Ben got its name. Some people think Big Ben was named for a British politician of the 1800s, Sir Benjamin Hall. His name is carved inside the bell.[3]

Big Ben might have been named for Benjamin Caunt, a big boxer from London. At six feet two inches, he was taller and heavier than most men.[4] People loved to watch Big Ben Caunt fight in the boxing ring.

We may never know the source of Big Ben's name. We do know Big Ben was created to ring in London's new tower called Palace of Westminster.

The clock tower would also be a challenge. Many people did not believe a clock could provide the right time. Village clocks often disagreed from village to village. This confused travelers. A man might think he had arrived for tea according to the clock in the village he left two hours earlier. Upon arriving in the second village, he was one hour late!

A British lawyer named Edmund Beckett Denison believed it was possible to build a village clock that could consistently tell the correct time. Denison loved clocks and studied how they were made.

He borrowed an idea from the famous sixteenth-century inventor Galileo Galilei. Once, in church, Galileo noticed a swinging lamp. He

Galileo Galilei

timed the lamp's swings. Each swing took the same amount of time, no matter how far from center the lamp traveled. Galileo called the swinging part of the clock a pendulum.

One hundred years later, in 1656, Dutch scientist Christiaan Huygens invented a pendulum clock. It included a piece called an escapement. This piece allowed the energy from the pendulum to "escape" evenly. It then allowed the pendulum to keep moving. Huygens' clocks lost only 15 seconds per day. Earlier clocks lost 15 minutes per day.[5]

Denison knew a pendulum and escapement would help Big Ben keep accurate time. He worked on the project with another British clockmaker named Edward John Dent. Dent had invented a way for ships to know the time when at sea.

Denison and Dent worked hard on the new clock and tower. The tower was called the Great Tower. The clock was called the Great Clock. Sadly, Dent died in 1853 before the projects were completed. Without his help, work on the clock tower slowed. People in London wondered, *Would the new clock tower ever be completed?*

After arriving at New Palace Yard, Big Ben had been placed in a gallows until the tower was completed. Each day someone used a hammer to check Big Ben's ring tone. It sounded loud and clear.

Then in 1857, the unthinkable happened. Big Ben cracked!

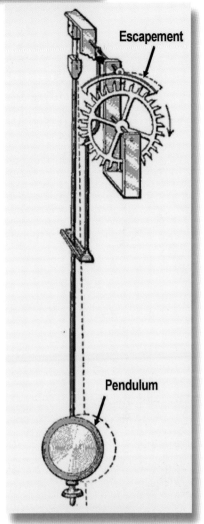

Escapement

Pendulum

Pendulum with escapement

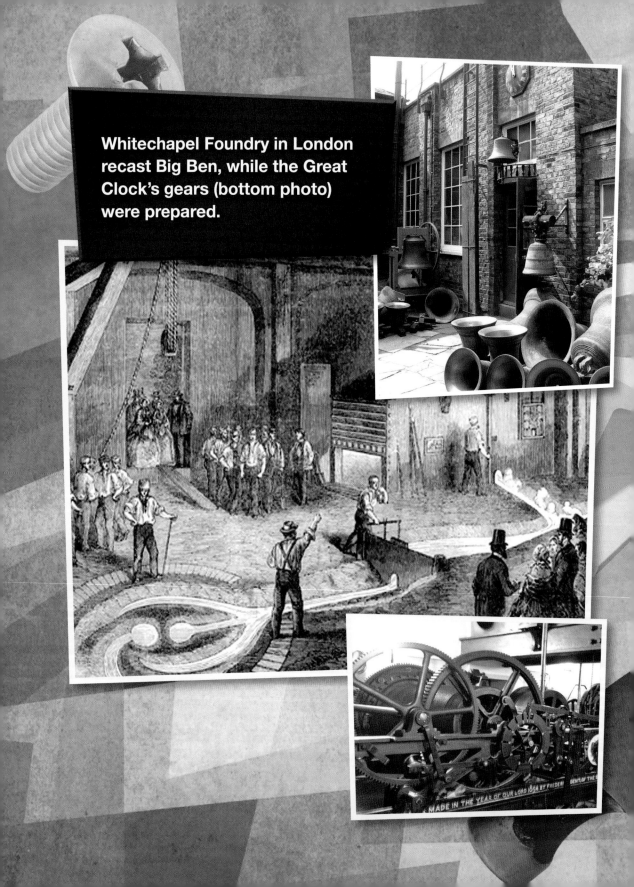

Whitechapel Foundry in London recast Big Ben, while the Great Clock's gears (bottom photo) were prepared.

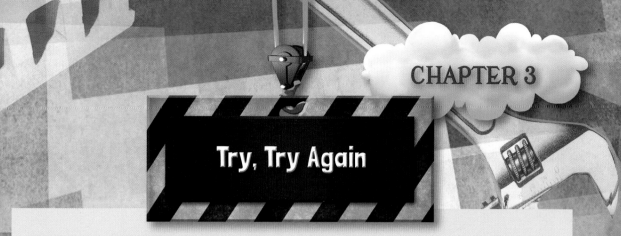

Try, Try Again

Big Ben's break stretched a miserable four feet.

Some people thought the hammer used to strike the bell was too heavy. Other people thought Big Ben was cursed.[1] Whatever the reason, the bell had to be repaired.

In 1858, workers took Big Ben to Whitechapel Bell Foundry in London. This foundry was well known. It had cast the Liberty Bell in Philadelphia.

Trained workers at the foundry examined Big Ben. The news was not good. The damage to Big Ben was too severe to be repaired. Another bell would have to be cast.

Using metal melted from the cracked bell, foundry workers carefully molded the new Big Ben. They didn't want to have another disaster with a too-heavy bell. When the mold was opened, the new bell looked perfect. Even better, it weighed less than 14 tons.[2]

They also made four smaller bells to hang in the tower with Big Ben. These would ring the quarter hours (every 15 minutes).

Meanwhile, work on the Great Clock continued. It would be huge and have four faces so that everyone in London could see the time. Each face measured 23 feet across. The numbers on each face reached two feet, while the minute hand stretched 16 feet![3]

Inside the clock were three sets of gears called trains. The going train moved the hands on the clock's faces. The chiming train made the quarter bells chime. The striking train pulled a cable, which caused Big Ben to chime.[4]

Chapter 3

The steps to Big Ben

Inside the Great Tower, its 334 steps twisted in a circle as they led 316 feet to the top.[5] Even at that height the Great Tower was not the tallest part of the Palace of Westminster. Victoria Tower, located at the other end and completed in 1858, stood 331 feet tall.

By October 1858, the tower and bell were ready. The smaller bells had easily been fit in place in September. When workers tried to hoist Big Ben to the belfry, the special room above the clock, they could not. The bell was too wide to fit through the tower.

The workers would not give up. With great care they turned the bell on its side. Securing it with ropes, they lifted the heavy bell hand over hand 200 feet to the belfry. It took them all day and all night. Finally, after 30 hours, Big Ben reached the top.[6]

Next came the Great Clock. The clock was not as wide as the bell, so it could easily be raised. But the clock had its own problems. The hour hands of gunmetal worked fine, but the minute hands of cast iron were too heavy. Workers replaced them with ones made of copper. These lighter hands worked well.

In May of 1859, the Great Clock started telling the time over London. In July, Big Ben began ringing the hours. Again the people of London cheered. It had been worth the wait for the new tower and bell to reign over their beloved city.

Their joy would not last. On October 1, 1859, disaster struck. Big Ben cracked again.

For three years Big Ben stayed silent. Many people, tired of the delays, wondered if a new clock tower would ever be part of London.

Someone voiced a suggestion. Why not simply turn the bell? The citizens of London thought about it. Could striking Big Ben at a different spot work? It was worth a try. To everyone's relief, Big Ben rang out clear.

Big Ben's loud gongs could be heard throughout the city. People loved to look up and hear the tones ring out.

On New Year's Eve in 1923, Big Ben became even more popular. A radio microphone was set up across the street. At midnight Big Ben's chimes rang in the New Year. The microphone carried the sounds to listeners. This was Big Ben's first time on the air, and it was a great success.

The tradition of ringing in the New Year continues today. Each year on December 31, people gather to hear Big Ben's chimes welcome the New Year.

Big Ben on New Year's Eve

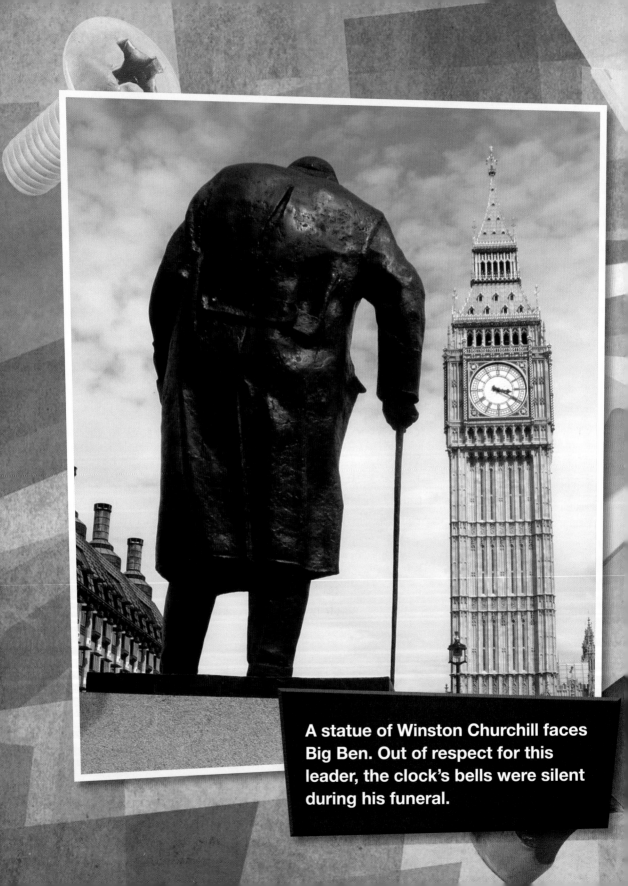

A statue of Winston Churchill faces Big Ben. Out of respect for this leader, the clock's bells were silent during his funeral.

Big Ben Rules

Big Ben has rung during sad times, too. In May of 1910, Big Ben tolled during King Edward VII's funeral. It did the same for the funerals of King George V in 1936 and King George VI in 1952.

Winston Churchill was a famous World War II leader in England. When he died in 1965, Big Ben's bells stayed silent out of respect.

Big Ben is also quiet on the second Sunday of each November. The day is called Remembrance Sunday. It is the date of the end of World War I. On that day people lay flowers on graves of soldiers. At 11 a.m. they are quiet for two minutes, then Big Ben begins ringing. Guns are fired into the air. These actions show respect for the British soldiers who died for their country.

During World War I (1914–1918) and World War II (1939–1945), Big Ben did more than tell time. It stood as a symbol of courage and hope for the people of England. When they felt afraid and discouraged about the attacks against their country, Big Ben's chimes cheered them. People around the world who heard Big Ben on the radio knew the people of England had not surrendered. Then, in May 1941, a bomb destroyed part of the Palace of Westminster. For many Londoners it was as though a member of the family had been attacked. Thankfully, Big Ben survived.

However, a link installed between the Great Clock and the Royal Observatory in Greenwich, England, was lost during the bombing. The Royal Observatory was known for having the most accurate time in the world. The link had been established to make sure the clock always

told the right time. Tests were run for several years after the war. It was finally decided that Big Ben could run on its own.

Big Ben's fortitude was so admired during the war that songwriters wrote songs about it: "Big Ben Is Saying Goodnight," "When Big Ben Chimes," and "The Big Ben Chime Waltz." An opera called *Big Ben* was written in 1946.

After 150 years, the Great Clock stays accurate with regular maintenance. People who care for it, called Keepers of the Clock, climb the stairs to the clock room three times each week, year-round. They clean the pendulum and check the trains. Each spring and fall, they adjust the clock's hands when the country's time changes for daylight savings.

If the clock slows, even for a fraction of a second, the clock keeper places a penny on the pendulum. This changes the center of gravity of the pendulum, making the clock go faster by two-fifths of a second.[1]

The Keepers of the Clock also care for the Ayrton Light at the very top of the tower. Installed in 1885, the light let the Queen know when government leaders were gathered in Parliament. The light was turned out when the

Keeping the clock includes keeping it clean.

leaders went home. It was named for Acton Smee Ayrton, a British government leader who thought of the idea. The Ayrton Light is still used today.[2] Other improvements to the tower over the years include gas jets behind the clock's dials to light the clock's faces at night. In the early 1900s, the jets were replaced by electric light bulbs.

Despite the special care, the clock, tower, or bell may need extra attention. In 1934, Big Ben sat silent for two months during repairs. Great Tom, the clock of St. Paul's cathedral, tolled in its place.

Sometimes weather is a problem. In 1962, heavy snowfall lay on the clock's hands. This caused the clock to ring in the New Year ten minutes late. Sometimes no one knows the reason why Big Ben stops suddenly. In 1997 the clock stopped, then started itself again. In May 2005 it happened again. Could it have been the heat? Temperatures in London that day reached 90 degrees, which rarely happens. The mystery was never solved.

The biggest disaster happened on August 5, 1976. The clock keeper walked in to the clock room—and stopped in shock. The room looked like a bomb had exploded!

The Ayrton Light glows at the top of Big Ben.

Big Ben has been part of England's history for more than 150 years.

Long Live Big Ben!

Twisted pieces of metal had been flung around the room. One piece was stuck in the ceiling. The clock keeper guessed that parts of the clock had worn out. During the night, pieces spun wildly through the area.

The damage would take months to repair.[1] Workers had a deadline. On May 4, 1977, the clock was to be inspected by the Queen of England! With a lot of work, the Palace of Westminster and its Clock Tower was ready for the royal visit.

By 1959, the Great Tower, Great Clock, and Big Ben had worked together for a century. The trio, which was often called just Big Ben, had faced many problems—fire, repairs, and attacks.

That year the people of London celebrated Big Ben at a special service. A crowd gathered at the foot of the tower, giving speeches and singing. A stone etched with notes about the service was placed at the tower.

In the summer of 2009, the people of England recognized Big Ben's 150th birthday with an even bigger festival. Thousands of people toured parts of the tower. Crowds viewed an eight-foot replica, complete with chimes like Big Ben. A computer program showed the inner workings of the tower. An actor dressed like Sir Benjamin Hall, the politician for whom the bell may have been named. He talked to visitors and answered questions about Big Ben. Children played a game about Big Ben, and the Guy Fox History Project gave out free books about Big Ben's history.[2]

Little Ben

In another part of London, people built an ice model of the tower. One area featured a 70-foot tower made of 500 bales of straw. Even the country of Hungary joined in the celebration. It built a clock tower made out of chocolate! Newspapers, TV, magazines, and radio stations from around the world reported on Big Ben's birthday events.

That winter, the celebration continued as 400 children drew pictures of Big Ben for a contest. Winners traveled to London to receive prizes at a special party. The winning design was used on the government's Christmas card.[3]

These were not the first shows of affection for Big Ben. In 1894, a 30-foot clock tower called Little Ben had been placed at Victoria train station. It stands there still.

In 2012, the tower received special recognition. To honor Queen Elizabeth's 60th year as monarch of England, the tower was renamed Elizabeth Tower.

Today, bells bigger than Big Ben ring in England. Great Paul of St. Paul's Cathedral in London weighs 16 tons. Great George of Liverpool Cathedral weighs 14 tons. Most people would agree that Big Ben, which weighs less than 14 tons, does not have to be the biggest bell to be the best.

Thousands of people from around the world visit London each year. Many of them take photos of themselves standing near Big Ben. Some stay until the hour hand reaches twelve, then they call home so that loved ones can hear the bell ring. When Big Ben's famous gong sounds, people stop to listen.

Big Ben might be the most famous landmark in England. Its picture is stamped on postcards, mugs, T-shirts, scarves, teapots, and even food. It has been featured in films: *The 39 Steps*, *101 Dalmatians*, and *Harry Potter and the Order of the Phoenix*.

The stars of *Harry Potter and the Order of the Phoenix* pose in front of Big Ben, which was featured in the film.

When some people look at Big Ben, they see a building that stood for courage under enemy fire. Others are proud of the tower that has been a part of England's history for more than 150 years. Still others admire its beauty and precision. No matter

the reason, Big Ben will continue to be admired as it stands tall and strong in one of the biggest cities in the world. It is a symbol of perseverance, patience, and belief in big dreams.

Long live Big Ben!

1300	Tower clocks using the escapement device become popular, especially in England.
1500	Galileo develops his pendulum theories.
1656	Christiaan Huygens invents the pendulum clock.
1834	The Palace of Westminster in London burns. A new government building is planned.
1836	A contest is held among British architects for designs for the new Houses of Parliament.
1843	Denison and Dent work on the clock tower for the Houses of Parliament.
1852	Queen Victoria officially opens the new Houses of Parliament, though the building is not completed.
1856	Big Ben is cast at a foundry in the English village of Stockton-on-Tees. Later that year, it arrives in London.
1857	Big Ben cracks.
1858	The second Big Ben is cast by Whitechapel Bell Foundry in London.
1859	Big Ben is raised to the belfry in the Great Tower. The Great Westminster Clock is installed in the room directly below the bell. Two months later, Big Ben strikes the hours. In September, the quarter bells are added. Big Ben cracks again.
1862	Big Ben is successfully rotated a quarter of the way around so that it can be struck on a new spot, away from its crack.
1863	An electromagnetic link is established between Big Ben and the Royal Observatory at Greenwich, England.
1870	The Palace of Westminster is completed.
1894	A 30-foot-tall clock tower called Little Ben is installed outside London's Victoria train station.
1910	Big Ben tolls during King Edward VII's funeral. The same thing happens for the funerals of King George V in 1936 and King George VI in 1952.

1939–1945   Big Ben survives a German bomb that destroys part of the House of Commons, and dozens of raids during World War II.

1959   The people of London celebrate the 100th birthday of the Great Clock of Westminster and Big Ben.

1965   Big Ben is silent out of respect for former Prime Minister Winston Churchill's funeral.

1976   The Great Clock stays silent for several months when many pieces fall apart from wear.

1977   The clock is restored in time for Queen Elizabeth's visit to the Houses of Parliament.

2009   The people of England celebrate Big Ben's 150th birthday with a yearlong series of events.

2012   The tower is renamed Elizabeth's Tower, commemorating the 60th anniversary of Queen Elizabeth's reign.

2015   Because of the subway running under the Houses of Parliament, Big Ben leans 18 inches off center. Major repairs to the whole Parliament building, costing billions of dollars, are scheduled to begin in 2020.

Chapter Notes

Chapter 1. King of Bells

1. Peter MacDonald, *Big Ben: The Bell, the Clock and the Tower* (Sparkford: Sutton, 2004), p. 38.
2. Ibid., p. 45.
3. Ibid., p. 37.
4. Ibid., p. 38.

Chapter 2. A Great Clock

1. Peter MacDonald, *Big Ben: The Bell, the Clock and the Tower* (Sparkford: Sutton, 2004), p. 23.
2. Chris McKay, *Big Ben: Great Clock and the Bells at the Palace of Westminster* (Oxford: Oxford University Press, 2010), p. 33.
3. MacDonald, p. 76.
4. Ibid., p. 77.
5. Jeremy Norman, "Huygens Invents the Pendulum Clock, Increasing Accuracy Sixty Fold," *History of Information,* June 26, 2015, http://www.historyofinformation.com/expanded.php?id=3506

Chapter 3. Try, Try Again

1. Peter MacDonald, *Big Ben: The Bell, the Clock and the Tower* (Sparkford: Sutton, 2004), p. 40.
2. Ibid., p. 43.
3. Ibid., p. 47.
4. Ibid., p. 46.
5. Ibid., p. 74.
6. Ibid., p. 45.

Chapter 4. Big Ben Rules

1. Kylie MacLellan, "150-Year-Old Pennies Removed from Big Ben," *Reuters,* November 12, 2009, http://www.reuters.com/article/2009/11/12/us-britain-bigben-idUSTRE5AB5MT20091112
2. "Clock Tower: Ayrton Light 1," Parliament.uk., n.d, accessed July 4, 2015, http://www.parliament.uk/visiting/online-tours/virtualtours/bigben-tour/

Chapter 5. Long Live Big Ben!

1. Associated Press, "Big Ben Mysteriously Stops Ticking," *Fox News,* May 28, 2005, http://www.foxnews.com/story/2005/05/28/london-big-ben-mysteriously-stops-ticking.html
2. "Big Ben's 150th Anniversary Year," Parliament.uk., n.d, accessed April 28, 2015, http://www.parliament.uk/about/living-heritage/building/palace/big-ben/building-clock-tower/150th-anniversary/
3. Peter MacDonald, *Big Ben: The Bell, the Clock and the Tower* (Sparkford: Sutton, 2004), p. 45.

Further Reading

Works Consulted

"Big Ben Goes Into Operation in London." History.com, 2009. Accessed April 28, 2015. http://www.history.com/this-day-in-history/big-ben-goes-into-operation-in-london

"Big Ben's 150th Anniversary Year." Parliament.uk., n.d. Accessed April 28, 2015. http://www.parliament.uk/about/living-heritage/building/palace/big-ben/building-clock-tower/150th-anniversary/

Cooke, Robert. *Palace of Westminster.* London: Burton Skira Ltd. 1987.

Darwin, John. *The Triumphs of Big Ben.* Suffolk: Robert Hale, 1986.

"Great Bells of the British Isles." *Tower Bells.* Accessed June 25, 2015. http://www.towerbells.org/data/GBGreatBells.html

Guy Fox History Project: "Happy Birthday, Big Ben!" Accessed June 22, 2015. http://bigbenfacts.co.uk/

"History of Big Ben." n.d. Accessed July 4, 2015. http://www.bigben.freeservers.com/history.html

Institution of Mechanical Engineers. *Big Ben: Its Engineering Past and Future.* Suffolk: D.M. Cornish & Company, 1981.

MacDonald, Peter. *Big Ben: The Bell, the Clock and the Tower.* Sparkford: Sutton, Publishing Limited, 2004.

McKay, Chris. *Big Ben: Great Clock and the Bells at the Palace of Westminster.* Oxford: Oxford University Press, 2010.

Norman, Jeremy. "Huygens Invents the Pendulum Clock, Increasing Accuracy Sixty Fold." *History of Information*, June 26, 2015. http://www.historyofinformation.com/expanded.php?id=3506

Oakley, Robin. "Big Ben Clocks Up 150 Year Anniversary." *CNN*, April 10, 2008. Accessed April 28, 2015. http://edition.cnn.com/2008/WORLD/europe/04/10/bigben.oakley/

Parliament. "Big Ben," n.d. Accessed June 22, 2015. http://www.parliament.uk/bigben

Rath, Kayte. "Big Ben's Tower Renamed Elizabeth Tower in Honour of Queen." *BBC News*, June 26, 2012, http://www.bbc.com/news/uk-politics-18592966

Secrets of Westminster. Directed by Louise Wardle. PBS, 2014. DVD.

Books

Formichelli, Linda. *Timekeeping: Explore the History and Science of Telling Time (Build It Yourself)*. White River Junction, VT: Nomad Press, 2012.

Koscielniak, Bruce. *About Time: A First Look at Time and Clocks.* New York: HMH Books for Young Readers, 2013.

Munro, Roxie. *The Inside-Outside Book of London.* New York: Universe Publishing, 2015.

On the Internet

Big Ben Facts for Kids.
     http://factsforkids.net/big-ben-facts-kids-exciting-8-facts-clock-tower/

Facts about Big Ben for Kids, The Free Resource.
     http://thefreeresource.com/facts-about-big-ben-for-kids

Guy Fox History Project: "Happy Birthday, Big Ben!"
     http://bigbenfacts.co.uk/

architect (AR-kih-tekt)—A person who designs large buildings.

belfry (BEL-free)—Part of a steeple or other structure in which a bell is hung.

center of gravity—The center of mass for an object; unsupported objects will fall over if their center of gravity leans beyond their base.

electromagnetic (ee-LEK-troh-mag-NEH-tik)—Using electricity to create a magnetic field.

escapement (es-KAYP-ment)—A mechanical device that controls the rate of moving gears in a clock by releasing the gears one notch at a time.

fortitude (FOR-tih-tood)—Strength of character.

gallows (GAL-ohs)—A wooden frame upon which something is hung.

minster (MIN-ster)—A large church that was usually part of a monastery (a place where religious men lived, worked, learned, and prayed.)

monarch (MAH-nark)—Ruler.

pendulum (PEN-joo-lum)—A swinging lever with a heavy bob that keeps time for a clock.

perseverance (per-seh-VEER-untz)—Maintaining a steady course of action in spite of difficulties or discouragement.

prime minister (prym-MIN-ih-ster)—Head of a country.

replica (REH-plih-kuh)—A close or exact copy.

schooner (SKOO-ner)—A small sailing vessel.

Ayrton Light 18-19

Big Ben
  admiration of 24, 25
  celebrations for 21, 22, 23
  cleaning of 18
  cracks of 11, 13, 14
  films featuring 23
  named for 9, 10
  renaming of 22
  repair of 13
  ringing for royalty funerals 17
  ringing on New Year's Eve of 15
  silent period of 15
  size of 4, 5, 7
  songs of 18
  transportation of 6
  weight of 7
  workings of 11, 13
  World Wars, service during 17

Caunt, Benjamin 10

chiming train 13

Churchill, Winston 16

Clock Keeper 18

Denison, Edmund Beckett 10, 11

Dent, Edward John 11

Elizabeth, Queen 21, 22

Galileo 10, 11

going train 13

Great Clock 11, 13, 14, 17, 18, 19, 21

Great George 22–23

Great Paul 9, 22

Great Peter 6

Great Tom 19

Great Tower 11, 14

Guy Fox History Project 21

Hall, Sir Benjamin 8, 9, 21

Harry Potter and the Order of the Phoenix 23

Huygens, Christiaan 11

Keepers of the Clock 18

London 5, 9

New Palace Yard 5, 9, 11

Palace of Westminster 9, 10, 14, 17, 21

Remembrance Sunday 17

River Thames 9

Royal Observatory 17

Stockton-on-Tees 5, 6, 7

striking train 13

Victoria, Queen 4, 5

Victoria Tower 14

Wave, The 6, 7

Whitechapel Bell Foundry 12, 13

Westminster Bridge 5